SECRETS IN
The Grand Canyon, Zion
and Bryce Canyon National Parks

Published by National Photographic Collections
North Palm Beach, Florida

SECRETS IN THE GRAND CANYON, ZION AND BRYCE CANYON NATIONAL PARKS

By Lorraine Salem Tufts

Photographs by Tom Bean, Peter & Alice Bengeyfield, Lynn Chamberlain, Mike Columbia, Walter Davidson, Jeff Foott, Michael Francis, Charles Gurche, Henry Holdsworth, Tracey Ingraham Holmes, Fred Joy, Rich Kirchner, K.D. McGraw, B. "Moose" Peterson, Trish Ramhorst, Doug Sokell & Lorraine Salem Tufts

Published by National Photographic Collections

Art Direction by Katie Pelisek & Lorraine Tufts

Design by Katie Pelisek

Editor and Contributing Writer, Tracey Holmes

Consulting Editors, Dr. Nicole Duplaix & Zoe Sanders

Geological Editor, Bruce Nelson

Historical Research, Tracey Ingraham Holmes

Published in the United States of America by:

National Photographic Collections
390 Golfview Road F, North Palm Beach
Florida 33408 USA
1-800-411-6144
1-561-626-3233
www.nationalphotocollections.com

Printed & Bound: Regent Publishing

Typography by Typo Graphics Inc, Orlando, FL
Set in: Winsor Light Condensed, Metro Black 2 & Berkeley Oldstyle Medium

Printed in China

Fourth Printing

Softcover & Hardcover

Fourth Edition
First Edition Copyright © 1992
Second Edition Copyright © 1994
Third Edition Copyright © 1998
Fourth Edition Copyright © 2005

National Photographic Collections

Library of Congress Cataloging in Publication Data
Tufts, Lorraine Salem, 1947-
   Secrets in the Grand Canyon, Zion and
   Bryce Canyon National Parks
   1. Grand Canyon, Zion and Bryce Canyon
Parks
      (Ariz., Utah)--Description--Photographic.
   I. Tufts, Lorraine Salem   II. Title
      . . 1992 . . 91-068053
Secrets in,# 2
ISBN 0-9620255-3-4   Softcover Edition
ISBN 0-9620255-4-2   Hardcover Edition

Acknowledgements

The author wishes to express her gratitude to: the staff of Grand Canyon National Park, especially to Greer Price, Information Specialist and Valerie L Meyer, Park Librarian, for their invaluable assistance and knowledge and to Nan Strickland for her help; the staff of Zion National Park, particularly Tmothy Manns, Chief Park Naturalist, Vic Vieira, Resource Manager, Rick Fedorchak, and Margaret Malm, the staff of Bryce Canyon National Park, especially Susan Colclazer, Chief of Interpretation, Dave Mecham, Ed Franzt, the staff of the Bryce Canyon Natural History Association, specifically LaKay Quilter and Paula Henre; Marcus Smith, Grand Canyon Expedition Company, Mike Denoyer, Linda Kollander, Jeanne Johnson and Marty Mathis; the Eastman Kodak Company, Dr. Nicole Duplaix, Mark Thompson, Zoe Sanders, Bruce Nelson, Sally Nelson, Ruth and Tom Austin, Mike Columbia, Bill Long, Katie, Steve and Daniel Pelisek; Bruce Bennett, Kit Law, Becky Lewis, Dominie Lenz, Steve of Trans Canyon Service, John Rich Jr. of Jacob's Lake Resort, Brewster, Helen, Brewster Jr. and Justin Boyd, Lilly of the Zion House, Eric Hallbeck, Barbara Brams, Tracey Ingraham Holmes and my darling Mother, Sophie M. Salem for their constant love and deep commitment as I struggled with various aspects of this project over the years. Marguerite I. Holmes for her generosity; to Susan Yeager for gripping for me and to my Mother and father for their love, support and interest.

Lorraine Salem Tufts　　　　　*Canon T90*
Canon 300mm 2.8 lens, 1/250sec. at f8
Monopod　　　　　*Kodachrome 64*

WESTERN BLUEBIRD

Photographed on the South Rim of Grand Canyon, this bird can be seen in all three parks.

Lorraine Salem Tufts　　　　　*Canon T-90*
Canon 300mm2.8lens, 1/250sec. at f8
Monopod　　　　　*Kodachrome 64*

PONDEROSA PINE WITH CONE

This conifer is found in all three parks.

Lorraine Salem Tufts　　　　　*Canon T90*
Canon 300mm 2.8 lens, 1/500sec. at f2.8
Monopod　　　　　*Kodachrome 64*

KAIBAB SQUIRREL

Cover Photographs: **GRAND CANYON** by Lorraine Salem Tufts, Canon T-90, 35-105mm lens, 1/180sec. at f9.5, Tripod, Fuji Velvia 50
ZION, MOONRISE AT SUNSET by Lorraine Salem Tufts, Canon EOS 5, 35-350mm lens, 1/10sec. at f16, Tripod, Fuji Velvia 50
THE HUNTER, BRYCE by Lorraine Salem Tufts, Canon EOS 5, 35-350mm lens, 1/4sec. at f16, Tripod, Fuji Velvia 50
Title Page Photograph: **MULE DEER** by Lorraine Salem Tufts, Canon T-90, 300mm2.8lens, 1/250sec. at f8, Monopod, Kodachrome 200

IN MEMORY OF

AUNT SALLY

And to all adults who take the time to unconditionally
love and care for a child.

Jeff Foott   *Nikon F2*   *Nikkor 300mm lens,*
1/60 sec. at f4   *Ball head with a clamp*   *Kodachrome 64*

GOSHAWK WITH YOUNG

Females are larger and stronger than the males, as is the case
with most birds of prey. Goshawks are listed as inhabiting the
Grand Canyon, Zion and Bryce Canyon National Parks.

4

Lorraine Salem Tufts   *Canon T-90*   *Canon 35-105mm 3.5 lens, 1/250 sec. at f8*
Polarizer   *Fuji Velvia 50*

LAVA FALLS RAPID

A Grand Canyon Expeditions' river boat prepares its course on this class ten rapid at mile 179.6 of the Colorado River.

Lorraine Salem Tufts *Canon T-90* *Canon 35-105mm 3.5 lens, 1/6 sec. at f16* *Tripod* *Polarizer* *Fuji Velvia 50*

BOAT MESA AND BRYCE AMPHITHEATER FROM SUNSET POINT

6

Lorraine Salem Tufts   *Canon T-90*
Canon 24 mm 2.8 lens, 1/4 sec. at f16   *Tripod*   *Fuji Velvia 50*

THE ZION NARROWS

The darkened walls of Navajo sandstone flank both sides of the Mountain of Mystery and the Virgin River in this photograph. When hiking into the Narrows, one must walk or wade in the cold river most of the time.

Introduction

Grand Canyon National Park is located in northwestern Arizona. Zion and Bryce Canyon National Parks are found in southwestern Utah. All three parks are within 120 miles of each other. Although visually very different and geologically distinctive, they are related by their rock formations. The uninterrupted layering of two billion years of geologic history is displayed in the composite of these parks. Grand Canyon holds evidence of the PreCambrian and Paleozoic eras in its depths. Zion contains the layering of middle geologic time, as represented in the Mesozoic era. The Bryce Canyon amphitheaters display the youngest rocks, dating back to the Cenozoic era. All three share similar characteristics of sedimentary layering, uplift and erosion. Our goal is to take the reader up through the geologic staircase as simply and concisely as possible.

Secrets in The Grand Canyon, Zion and Bryce Canyon National Parks captures the essence of these areas in its photographic illustrations of the familiar and not so familiar. A great deal of attention has been given to the plants and animals, including birds and reptiles, who inhabit one or more of these parks. Large, fast telephoto lenses have been used whenever possible to magnify the animals, thereby offering them comfortable and necessary distances. Unusual light conditions, rainbows, lightning and other natural phenomena are especially featured. Haze-free scenics were a goal in photographing the canyons, often captured by waiting for rain and snow storms to clear the air.

Scientists, historians and writers have contributed their knowledge to our text. One chapter is devoted to each park with geological and historical sections included. Eighteen wildlife photographers exhibit some of their best work with the photo equipment and settings noted under each picture.

The varied natural wonders of these parks go far beyond what we have attempted to represent in this volume. Nonetheless, our deep appreciation of the treasures they offer can be seen in each of the 168 photographs cameoed in this collection of Grand Canyon, Zion and Bryce Canyon National Parks.

Lorraine Salem Tufts
1/350 sec. at f6.7

Canon T-90

Canon 100mm macro lens with extension tube,
Kodachrome 200

PHLOX
Various species of phlox are found in all three parks.

8

Lorraine Salem Tufts   *Canon T-90*   *Canon 35-105mm lens, 7/10 of a sec. at f16*
Polarizer   *Tripod*   *Fuji Velvia 50*

MOUNT HAYDEN FROM PT. IMPERIAL, NORTH RIM

The warm hues of the setting sun intensify the colors of Mount Hayden's Coconino sandstone and red Hermit shale, along with other Grand Canyon features illustrated here.

Grand Canyon National Park

Tom Bean   Pentax 6x7   55mm lens, 1/8 sec. at f11   Tripod   Fuji Velvia 50

RAINBOW OVER YAKI POINT, SOUTH RIM

"The Grand Canyon fills me with awe. It is beyond comparison—beyond description, absolutely unparalleled throughout the wide world. Let this great wonder of nature remain as it is now. Do nothing to mar its grandeur, sublimity and loveliness. You can not improve on it. But what you can do is keep it for your children, your children's children, and all who come after you, as the one great sight which every American should see. Don't let them skin this wonderful country —as they will try to do."

Theodore Roosevelt, May 6, 1903

The Geological Story

The Grand Canyon is an awesome wonder of nature. Vastly expansive with depths reaching roughly one mile, its sheer size intimidates some, while excites and challenges others. Ultimately, it evokes respect from all for its immensity, varied shapes and ever-changing colors. The interminable process of erosion stirs the imagination of anyone who gazes at the Canyon for the first time. The Grand Canyon is Earth's superb monument to time, erosion and uplift. The Colorado River has carved this natural wonder over the last six million years with rain, snow, sleet, hail and gravity widening its expanse. The rocks that compose the different formations of the Grand Canyon are much, much older.

To describe concisely the monumental processes that created and carved the Canyon, we will focus on ten major geologic phases. Most of these occurred long before the Grand Canyon and Colorado River existed. Geologists have estimated the beginnings and endings of most of these phases and processes. Nevertheless, the picture is quite clear except for some missing links and incomplete theories. For the most part, the exposed rock formations have an orderly tale of geologic time to tell.

About two billion years ago during the early Precambrian era, the first geologic phase in the story of the Grand Canyon region occurred. An accumulation of sediments and volcanic substances became horizontally layered for thousands of feet. Three hundred million years later, a second major phase began. The Earth's crust uplifted intermittently over the ages as a result of tectonic plate activity, creating a range of mountains probably five to six miles high. As the plates moved, tremendous pressure and heat recrystallized the rocks, and they metamorphosed into a formation known as Vishnu schist. Later, molten material forced its way into the rock, cooled and then hardened into Zoroaster granite. These two formations make up the walls of the Inner Gorge seen from different places on the rims of the Canyon.

For two hundred million years, erosion gnawed away at these mountains until they reduced to a plain. The sea invaded the lowering area, depositing the Grand Canyon Supergroup, a classification of the next nine rock formations. Many different environmental conditions created the varied sediments in the layers. These activities went on for 300 million years, until about 1.2 billion years ago.

Scientists believe that life existed on the planet

Lorraine Salem Tufts, Canon T-90, Canon 35-105mm 3.5 lens, 1/180 sec. at f9.5, Polarizer, Monopod on drifting boat, Fuji Velvia 50

ROCK FORMATIONS

This picture displays sedimentary rock formations from the Paleozoic era.

almost two billion years ago, although no traces have been found dating back that far in the Grand Canyon. The earliest known life recorded in these rocks can be found in the Bass limestone, the oldest layer of the Grand Canyon Supergroup. Deposited above the surface of the Vishnu group, the limestone layers were once, in part, the remains of primitive algae now fossilized as stromatolites.

Our story continues about 800 million years later when more movement occurred beneath the Earth's crust. This movement caused a range of fault-block mountains to occur slowly over time. Some areas of the mountains separated from the sheer force of this process, causing blocks to lift and tilt while others were lowered. As the mountains rose, erosion continued its relentless course. After

approximately 100 million years, the mountains eroded down to plains with more resistant areas left as hills. In some places the entire 12,000 foot thickness of the Supergroup eroded until the Vishnu group underneath was exposed. In other areas, this late Precambrian formation actually tilted and the rocks are still visible.

The next major geologic phase of the Grand Canyon region began when sediment was deposited during the Paleozoic era, roughly 600 to 230 million years ago. The Grand Canyon area again experienced varied environmental conditions which created different types of sedimentary deposits. Sandstone, siltstone, shale, limestone and dolomite are all that remain of ancient seas, river flood plains and vast deserts.

Starting about 600 million years ago, the first rock layer of the Paleozoic era, the Tapeats sandstone, slowly accumulated. In some areas this sandstone layer rests directly above the Vishnu group, creating a gap in the geologic record known as the Great Unconformity. Erosion created this and other unconformities throughout the Paleozoic era, erasing the previously existing rock layer.

Above the Tapeats layer lies the Bright Angel shale formation. Consisting primarily of shale and green sandstone, it forms a vast greenish platform above the Inner Gorge known as the Tonto Plateau. The composition of the rock in this formation acts as an aquiclude or barrier to the downward movement of groundwater. Little surface water remains on either of the rims. Instead, water in the form of rain and snow seeps downward into the porous layers of rock. The water continues to travel downward until it reaches the relatively dense rocks of the Bright Angel shale. Then, it is forced horizontally, through the younger Muav formation, to the surface. There it exits as beautiful springs in the canyon walls.

The youngest rock layer in the Tonto group, the Muav, was made of marine-deposited limestone. It distinguishes itself from the Bright Angel shale as an aquifer rather than a barrier to water seeping downward. All three of these formations—the Tapeats, Bright Angel and Muav—sandwich various fossils within their layers.

Millions of years ago, the land rose above the sea, and was eventually eroded, creating another unconformity. This left a geological gap between the Muav formation and its successor, Temple Butte, which is known for its distinctive fossils of animals with backbones. Above the Temple Butte formation rest the impressive layers of the Redwall limestone. The red color on the surface of the limestone comes from the iron oxide bleeding down from the Supai formation above. Without the iron oxide, this formation is actually gray in color.

After the Redwall limestone formation was deposited, erosion again created another gap in the geologic record. Consequently, the Supai group of formations was deposited directly above the Redwall layer. Again a shallow retreating sea set the stage for the lower formations in this grouping. Abundant life remains are found in both the Redwall formation and the Supai group.

Scientists hypothesize that the sediments which comprise the upper portion of the Supai group were deposited by rivers with plants along their banks. Animals, perhaps looking something like alligators or crocodiles, also lived in and around the water. Separated by another unconformity, the Supai group sits just below the Hermit shale formation which is also red in color. Freshwater streams, which once carried mud and clay, deposited the iron oxide. These layers reveal that winged insects, cone-bearing plants and ferns all thrived in the semi-arid climate of this period.

Directly above the Hermit shale formation, layers of Coconino sandstone were formed from sediments occurring during a desert-like period. Reptiles and insects inhabited the area and evidence of their existence is preserved in these rock layers. Another warm sea replaced the former desert environment, creating the younger rocks of the Toroweap formation. Red and yellow sandstone distinguish this 250 foot formation. Marine life flourished during this geologic period as evidenced by the brachiopod and mollusk fossils.

The Kaibab limestone, the youngest rock formation in the Paleozoic era, was deposited by an advancing sea. It left the remains of sea creatures, including shark's teeth, behind. The creamy white layers of this formation are on both rims. Remnants of several younger formations from the Mesozoic era, the eighth major geologic phase occurring 230 to 65 million years ago, also exist in Grand Canyon National Park.

Sometime around 65 million years ago, the ninth major geologic phase began with the gradual and intermittent uplift of the Colorado Plateau and the erosion of the Mesozoic era rock formations. During this time, the area now known as the Grand Canyon rose approximately 9000 feet. Most of the Mesozoic era rock, of which Zion National Park is a good example, has been eroded except for some remaining deposits. The relatively young rocks of the Mesozoic or "Dinosaur Era" have long since been erased from the geologic record of the Grand Canyon, leaving a sobering reminder of just how ancient the rock is below our feet.

About six million years ago during the Cenozoic era, the tenth and most recent major geological phase began when what is now called the Colorado River became a formidable erosive force sweeping across the Kaibab Plateau. The river's erosive process was assisted by rain, snow, gravity and time. Eventually these forces of nature shaped the deep canyons which we see in the park today.

A little more than one million years ago, volcanos spewed lava down the canyon walls. The lava dammed up the river, forming lakes. After thousands of years of erosion and carving, the river broke through the natural barriers, leaving great rapids such as Lava Falls behind.

The tenth major geologic phase is ongoing. Erosion still plays the most significant role in the continuing formation and shaping of the Grand Canyon. As the 4.6 billion year old geologic story of the Earth continues, the revealing layers of Grand Canyon National Park will always be a testament to the grand forces of nature.

Lorraine Salem Tufts, Canon T-90, Canon 24mm 2.8 lens, 1/10 sec. at f16, Polarizer, Tripod, Kodachrome 64

Lorraine Salem Tufts, Canon T-90, Canon 35-105mm 3.5 lens, 1/250 sec. at f8, Monopod on a drifting boat, Fuji Velvia 50

Lorraine Salem Tufts, Canon T-90, Canon 35-105mm 3.5 lens, 1/250 sec. at f8, Monopod on drifting boat, Fuji Velvia 50

THE VISHNU GROUP IN THE INNER GORGE AND COLORADO RIVER

THE GREAT UNCONFORMITY

Unconformities are geologic gaps in the sequence of rocks caused by erosion. In this picture, Tapeats sandstone was deposited directly on the older Precambrian rocks.

VISHNU SCHIST WITH VEINS OF ZOROASTER GRANITE

The History of Humans

12

Human history in the Grand Canyon has been a continuous struggle to understand and adapt to the environment of one of the most overwhelming natural features of this world. Centuries of Indian cultures, missionaries, explorers, river runners and tourists have all contributed their part to the comparatively brief, but significant period of human existence in the history of the Grand Canyon.

Archaeologists have traced man's history in this region as far back as 4,000 years. Several human artifacts, specifically split-twig animal figurines, have been found since the 1930s in limestone caves of the inner canyon area. Radiocarbon dating has enabled scientists to pinpoint that these figurines, only a few inches high, are 3,000 to 4,000 years old. Due to this and other evidence, historians now believe that these early canyon dwellers may have been part of the Desert Culture, characterized by seminomadic Indians who hunted and foraged for their survival.

From approximately B.C. 500 to A.D 1150, another Indian culture named the Anasazi occupied the rims and inner canyon area. The first Anasazis to inhabit the area were the Basketmaker Indians, descendants of their Desert Culture predecessors. Named because of their adept basket making abilities, these people survived primarily by hunting and foraging, supplemented by limited crop development. They lived in small communal bands sheltered by caves or circular mud houses. Around A.D. 500 the Anasazi culture began to develop in a more complex manner when new varieties of agriculture made life more stable.

At the same time as the Anasazi culture began to flourish in the eastern portion of the Grand Canyon, another group of Indians called the Cohonina inhabited the area west of what is now Grand Canyon Village. Although influenced by their Anasazi neighbors, the Cohonina did distinguish themselves as a separate cultural entity.

By A.D. 800 the Anasazi of the Grand Canyon began using stones, along with mud and poles, to construct above-ground living quarters. Referred to as the "Pueblo" period, these Indians would seasonally migrate from the river deltas of the canyon floor in the winter to the high plateaus in the hot summer months. Extensive agricultural fields and granaries to store the harvest were maintained along with nearby multi-roomed pueblos.

Both the Anasazi and Cohonina appeared to have flourished until mid-A.D. 1100 as exemplified by the thousands of archaeological sites in the Canyon which date back to this time period. However, no trace of their existence can be found after A.D. 1200. According to scientists, dramatic changes in the climate and accompanying drought forced the Cohonina and Anasazi from the North and South Rims to leave the area in search of a more favorable environment.

Approximately one hundred years passed before the next group of Indians came to occupy the Grand Canyon. Two tribes, the Paiute from the east and the Cerbat from the west, eventually reoccupied the plateaus and inner canyons of the region. While the Paiute inhabited the plateaus north of the Colorado River, the Cerbat occupied a large part of the Coconino Plateau on the South Rim where Grand Canyon Village is now located. Like their Anasazi predecessors, both Indian cultures adapted well to the environment, and consequently remained a stable community in the area until the U.S. Army

Walter Davidson   Nikon FM2   Nikkor 35-200mm lens, 1/250 sec. at f5.6   Kodachrome 64

PETROGLYPHS

Petroglyphs are rock carvings found throughout canyon country. This example was found outside the park.

moved them onto reservations in 1882. The Havasupai and Hualapai Indians are descendants of the Cerbat, and both still occupy lands given to them adjacent to Grand Canyon National Park.

Even though several different Indian cultures had inhabited the Grand Canyon since at least B.C. 2000, the first documented European encounter with the Grand Canyon did not occur until A.D. 1540 when a party of Spanish soldiers, under the command of Garcia Lopez de Cardenas, set out with Hopi guides to find the "great western river." The party found the Colorado River, but actually descending to it was another matter. They abandoned attempts to reach the river after three days, never descending farther than one-third of the way down the canyon walls. The next Spanish expedition did not return to the Canyon until over 200 years later in 1776, when Father Francisco Tomas Garces successfully traveled east along the South Rim of the Grand Canyon, encountering the Havasupai and other Indians.

In 1848 the United States government finally acquired the lands of the Grand Canyon region under the treaty of Guadalupe Hidalgo after the successful Mexican War. Interest in the potential natural resources of the region inspired several government expeditions, including one of the most interesting in 1857-1858 under the direction of Lt. Joseph Ives. Although Ives recognized the inherent beauty of the region, he thought that the area was "altogether valueless" and pessimistically hypothesized that his expedition would be "doubtless. . .the last party of whites to visit this profitless locality."

In stark contrast to Ives' evaluation of the area, Major John Wesley Powell, a learned scientist and avid explorer, found immeasurable aesthetic and scientific value in the Grand Canyon. In 1869 Major Powell led nine men on a heroic and invaluable journey down the Colorado River through the Grand Canyon which he described as "the most sublime spectacle on earth." During the voyage Powell took systematically detailed notes on the rock formations, wildlife and Indian ruins among other things. These notes did a great deal to focus public attention on this unknown and spectacular region.

Following Powell's ground breaking exploration of the Grand Canyon, Clarence Dutton, an articulate and philosophical writer/scientist, added important insights to the ever increasing body of

Lorraine Salem Tufts   *Canon T-90*
35-105mm lens, 1/60 sec. at f4   Tripod   50FV

ANASAZI GRANARIES AT NANKOWEAP

Tracey Ingraham Holmes   *Canon AE1P*
24mm 2.8 lens, 1/30 sec. at f13   Tripod   64K

ANASAZI RUINS ALONG THE COLORADO RIVER

Lorraine Salem Tufts   *Canon AE1P*
35-105mm 3.5 lens, 1/250 sec. at f8   64K

SUPPLIES ARRIVE AT PHANTOM RANCH

information about the region. During the years of 1880-1881, he conducted the first in-depth geological study for the recently formed U.S. Geological Survey. His detailed geological descriptions of the Grand Canyon along with pictures painted by Thomas Moran and William Henry Holmes were published in a report entitled *A Tertiary History of The Grand Canyon District*. The work, which added philosophical as well as geological understanding to this subject matter, also helped to increase the Canyon's notoriety.

While scientific exploration was making great strides in understanding the geology of the Grand Canyon, prospectors were interested in its geology for other reasons. The 1870s and 1880s were a time of mining fever in which individuals envisioned economic prosperity. Claims were staked in the Grand Canyon with the hopes that the deposits of lead, zinc, asbestos and copper which had been discovered would prove profitable. However, the problems of access into the Canyon and the difficulty of extracting the metal ore out of the rocks negated any real profit potential.

Coinciding with the decline in mining prospects was the increased national interest in conservation of natural resources at the turn of the century. This burgeoning national sentiment brought to the forefront the issue of natural resource conservation in which aesthetics were pitted against economic utility. This heightened awareness and shift in national priorities opened the way for a new era of tourism. It also laid the foundation for a system of national park conservation.

One tangible response to the economic shift toward tourism and away from mining was the development of plans for what was to become Grand Canyon Village. Although stage coaches had been bringing tourists into the area since 1883, the 1901 completion of the Santa Fe railroad line into Grand Canyon Village ushered in a new era of increased tourist visitation. The grand El Tovar hotel was finished in 1905, and such tourist facilities as Babbits, the Hopi House and Verkamps were soon to follow. New hiking trails were constructed along the older Indian trails and by 1903 one could hike from the North Rim all the way to the bottom of the canyon.

Increased visitation and public interest was a precursor to government protection. In 1903 President Theodore Roosevelt, a resolute advocate of national conservation, visited the Grand Canyon. He described it as "the most impressive piece of scenery I have ever looked at," and three years later established the Grand Canyon Game Preserve. The preserve became a mixed blessing for the area — reducing livestock overgrazing while at the same time eliminating natural predators such as wolves, eagles and cougars. Two years later, in 1908, Roosevelt designated the Game Preserve and already existing national forest a national monument. That status remained for eleven years until Grand Canyon became a park in 1919.

Development occurred above and below the rims during the time period between monument and national park status. The Kolb brothers who built a photographic studio on the edge of the South Rim were busy recording the grand panoramic images of the Canyon for the world. On the North Rim in 1917, the first rustic accommodations were opened by W. W. Wylie at Bright Angel Point to hostel interested visitors.

On February 26, 1919, nearly 40 years after Senator Benjamin Harrison of Indiana had intro-duced a bill to create Grand Canyon National Park, President Wilson signed the official legislation. This new park status did much to add to the development and notoriety of the area. Approximately nine years later, rim to rim access was made possible with the North Kaibab suspension bridge across the Colorado. In the same year, the architecturally aesthetic North Rim Lodge was constructed out of Kaibab limestone to blend into the Canyon's natural surroundings. Finally in 1935, the road along the South Rim of the Grand Canyon was completed. The facilities were ready and waiting to be used by the many tourists who would come to gaze into the depths of Grand Canyon's glory.

A further expansion of Grand Canyon National Park occurred under the important 1975 enactment in which President Gerald Ford doubled the size to its present day 1,892 square miles. Also under the enactment, the Havasupai Indians were given back thousands of acres of their original land in Havasu Canyon.

The history of Grand Canyon National Park is by no means a static one. Just as the geologic formations and processes evolve, so too do the chapters of man's history in the region. Park administrators have constantly been faced with new and difficult problems: the effects of Glen Canyon Dam on the Grand Canyon ecosystem, increased park visitation on the rims and on the Colorado River, and more recently, air quality problems from different sources; yet to each problem there are at least temporary solutions. Most important, there is worldwide recognition and reverence for this natural wonder. As more people experience the intricacies of its geology, wildlife and archaeology, the greater its intrinsic value to present and future generations will become.

14

Lorraine Salem Tufts   *Canon T-90*   *Canon 35-105mm 3.5 lens, 1/250 sec. at f8*   *Polarizer*   *Fuji Velvia 50*

GRAND CANYON EXPEDITIONS RIVER BOAT AT LAVA FALLS

About 277 miles of the Colorado River wind their way through Grand Canyon National Park, with many exciting rapids on the journey. Lava Falls is one of the most notable because it is a class ten rapid on a scale from one to ten. Remains of a volcanic lava flow that occurred about a million years ago created this rapid.

Lorraine Salem Tufts   *Canon T-90*   *Canon 35-105mm 3.5 lens,*
1/180 sec. at f9.5   *Polarizer*   *Fuji Velvia 50*

THE COLORADO RIVER AND OLDER PRECAMBRIAN ROCK

Lorraine Salem Tufts   *Canon T-90*   *35-105mm*
3.5 lens, 1/45 sec. at f8   *Tripod*   *Fuji Velvia 50*

SACRED DATURA

This sacred datura remains open during the early morning light at Trinity Creek on the Colorado River.

16

| Tom Bean | Canon F1 | 80-200mm lens, 8 secs. at f4 | Tripod | Kodachrome 64 |

LIGHTNING STRIKES AS SEEN FROM POINT IMPERIAL, NORTH RIM

At 8803 feet, Point Imperial, one of the highest overlooks in the park, serves as a dangerous but excellent vantage point for catching lightning strikes. A long exposure is the key to capturing successful lightning photographs at night.

Lorraine Salem Tufts   *Canon T-90*   *Canon 24mm 2.8 lens, 1 sec. at f16*   *Polarizer*   *Tripod*   *Fuji Velvia 50*

WATCHTOWER WITH THE COLORADO RIVER, SOUTH RIM

Mary Elizabeth Jane Colter, an architect for the Fred Harvey Company from 1902 to 1948, designed the watchtower at Desert View. The structure, built in 1933, perches on the South Rim of the Grand Canyon. Colter also designed Hermit's Rest, Phantom Ranch, Hopi House and Bright Angel Lodge in the park.

Lynn Chamberlain   *Nikon F3*
300mm 2.8 lens, 1/500 sec. at f4,   *Tripod*   *Kodachrome 64*

BOBCATS

Bobcats are fairly common in the Grand Canyon area and are also listed in Zion and Bryce Canyon National Parks, but sightings are uncommon.

Jeff Foott   *Nikon F4*
400mm lens, 1/125 sec. at f5.6   *Tripod*   *Kodachrome 64*

COYOTE PEEKING AROUND ROCK

Coyotes are not frequently seen by visitors, although they do live in all three parks. This one was photographed at morning's first light.

Lorraine Salem Tufts
Monopod

Canon EOS 5

Canon 300 mm lens, w/2x extender 1/500 sec. at f5.6
Fuji Provia100

CALIFORNIA CONDOR IMMATURE IN FLIGHT

On the 5th of November 2003, two captive-produced Califorina Condors released in northern Arizona produced a young that successfully fledged in the Grand Canyon. This is the first known occurrence of this event in over twenty years. The largest and most endangered raptor in the United States was released from a captive breeding program in 1996 in Arizona. This condor marked with the number seventy two is a male.

20

Lorraine Salem Tufts *Canon T-90* *Canon 300mm 2.8 lens,*
1/250 sec. at f5.6 *Monopod* *Kodachrome 200*

MULE DEER

Two males browse on catclaw growing at Phantom Ranch in the bottom of the Grand Canyon. Visitors commonly see mule deer throughout the Grand Canyon, Zion and Bryce Canyon National Parks.

Lorraine Salem Tufts
Canon 300mm 2.8 lens, 1/180 sec. at f6.7   *Monopod*   *Canon T-90*
Fuji Velvia 50

DESERT BIGHORN SHEEP RAM

Desert bighorn sheep arrived in the Southwest about 9,000 to 12,000 years ago according to fossil and archeological evidence. They are the most common animal represented in petroglyphs and pictographs during prehistoric times in the Southwest. The photographer found these along the Colorado River just below Deer Creek. Fewer numbers of these animals can also be found in Zion National Park.

22

Lorraine Salem Tufts *Canon T-90* *Canon 35-105mm 3.5 lens, 1/10 sec. at f16*
Polarizer *Tripod* *Kodachrome 25*

DEER CREEK FALLS

Located at mile 136 of the Colorado River, this beautiful falls has carved its way through layers of
Tapeats sandstone.

Lorraine Salem Tufts   *Canon T-90*   *Canon 24mm 2.8 lens, 1/2 sec. at f16*   *Tripod*   *Kodachrome 25*

INSIDE REDWALL CAVERN
Water has carved out the enormous Redwall Cavern, located in Marble Canyon at mile 33 of the Colorado River. Taken from the inside back wall of the cavern, the photographer has created an unusual composition contrasting blackness and the Canyon walls.

24

Lorraine Salem Tufts
Canon 300mm 2.8 lens, 1/125 sec. at f4   *Monopod*   *Canon T-90*
                                                                      Kodachrome 200

Lorraine Salem Tufts
Canon 300mm 2.8 lens, 1/250 sec. at f2.8   *Monopod*   *Canon T-90*
                                                                          Kodachrome 200

KAIBAB SQUIRREL, NORTH RIM

The Kaibab squirrel lives nowhere else in the world but on the Kaibab Plateau of the North Rim. A resident of the pine forest, this white-tailed, tassel-eared squirrel feeds primarily on ponderosa pine seeds and inner bark. Listed as rare and endangered, its closest relation is the Abert squirrel found on the South Rim.

Lorraine Salem Tufts
Canon 300mm 2.8 lens, 1/250 sec. at f5.6   *Monopod*   *Canon T-90*
                                                                       Kodachrome 64

Lorraine Salem Tufts
Canon 300mm 2.8 lens, 1/180 sec. at f4   *Monopod*   *Canon T-90*
                                                                       Kodachrome 25

ABERT SQUIRREL, SOUTH RIM

The Abert squirrel lives on the South Rim, and can also be found in Colorado and Mexico. These squirrels are similar in looks and coloration to the Kaibab, except for their tails and undersides. The Kaibab probably became isolated on the North Rim as the climate grew more arid around the higher elevation pine forests and as the Canyon widened over millions of years.

26

Henry H. Holdsworth   Wista 4x5   Nikkor 135mm 5.6 lens, 1/8 sec. at f4.5   Tripod   Fujichrome Velvia 50

TOROWEAP POINT AND THE COLORADO RIVER
AT SUNRISE, NORTH RIM
This North Rim point overlooking the Colorado River aptly exemplifies the powerful, erosive force of water.

Tracey Ingraham Holmes   *Canon AE1P*   *Canon 35mm 3.5 lens, 1/8 sec. at f16*   *Polarizer*   *Tripod*   *Kodachrome 25*

SUNSET ON THE GRAND CANYON
FROM THE SOUTH RIM

Lorraine Salem Tufts   *Canon T-90*   *Canon 300mm 2.8 lens, 1/250 sec. at f3.5*   *Kodachrome 64*

IMMATURE PEREGRINE FALCON

Federally listed as endangered, the peregrine falcon is making a strong recovery because of captive breeding and release programs established in 1970.

Henry H. Holdsworth
Nikkor 400mm 3.5 lens, 1/250 sec. at f8   *Bogen window mount*

Nikon FE2
Kodachrome 64

WILD TURKEY ON THE NORTH RIM

Wild turkeys were introduced to the Kaibab Plateau in 1950. Males are larger and far more color-ful than the females. The males' iridescent feathers are particularly impressive when they display their strutting posture.

Henry H.Holdsworth   *Nikon FE2*
Nikkor 600mm f4 lens with a 1.4x teleconverter, 1/500 sec. at f5.6   *Kodachrome 64*

BALD EAGLE

A species rarely seen in the Grand Canyon and federally listed as endangered, bald eagles can also be found in Bryce Canyon and Zion National Parks. This particular eagle landed along Marble Canyon for its usual look around. A patient photographer was ready and waiting with the afternoon sunlight warming the composition.

Lorraine Salem Tufts   *Canon T-90*   *Canon 150-600mm lens,*
1/125 sec. at f5.6   *Tripod*   *Fujichrome 100*

GOLDEN EAGLE

Usually spotted soaring in the air, golden eagles nest on cliffs and feed mainly on rabbits and large rodents. This species can be found in all three parks.

Lorraine Salem Tufts
1/500 sec. at f5.6

Canon T-90
Monopod

Canon 300mm 2.8 lens,
Kodachrome 64

GREAT BLUE HERON

These birds frequently can be seen fishing or sunning themselves along the Colorado River and its tributaries.

Lorraine Salem Tufts
1/250 sec. at f2.8

Canon T-90
Monopod

Canon 300mm 2.8 lens,
Kodachrome 64

AMERICAN AVOCET IN FLIGHT ALONG THE COLORADO RIVER

Although much smaller than the great blue heron, the American avocet is a large shorebird with long legs and a long upcurved bill. This species is uncommon in the Grand Canyon and Zion, and not found at all in Bryce.

Lorraine Salem Tufts   *Canon T-90*   *Canon 24mm 2.8 lens, 1/15 sec. at f16*   *Polarizer*   *Tripod*   *Fuji Velvia 50*

A VIEW OF THE COLORADO RIVER FROM MILE 52

The muddy Colorado River meanders its way down past the Bright Angel shale, Muav and Red-wall limestones. The Nankoweap formation, composed of a thick, purplish marine sandstone, can be seen in Nankoweap Canyon near here.

34

Tom Bean   Canon F1   80-200mm lens,
1/125 sec. at f5.6   Tripod   Kodachrome 64

**G R A N D   C A N Y O N
R A T T L E S N A K E**

Lorraine Salem Tufts   Canon T-90   Canon 300mm
2.8 lens, 1/750 sec. at f4   Monopod   Fuji Velvia 50

**D E S E R T   S P I N Y   L I Z A R D
E Y E I N G   I N S E C T**

Lorraine Salem Tufts   Canon T-90   Canon 300mm
2.8 lens, 1/250 sec. at f3.5 Monopod Kodachrome 64

G O P H E R   S N A K E

Lorraine Salem Tufts   Canon T-90   Canon 300mm 2.8 lens,
1/1000 sec. at f4.5   Monopod   Kodachrome 64

C O L L A R D   L I Z A R D

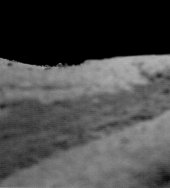

Lorraine Salem Tufts   Canon T-90   Canon 300mm 2.8 lens,
1/125 sec. at f2.8   Monopod   Kodachrome 64

M A L E   C H U C K W A L L A

The pink-colored Grand Canyon rattlesnake, a subspecies of the western rattlesnake, can only be
found in the Grand Canyon. Both the desert spiny lizard and the chuckwalla are found in Zion
but not Bryce, while the collard lizard and gopher snake live in all three parks.

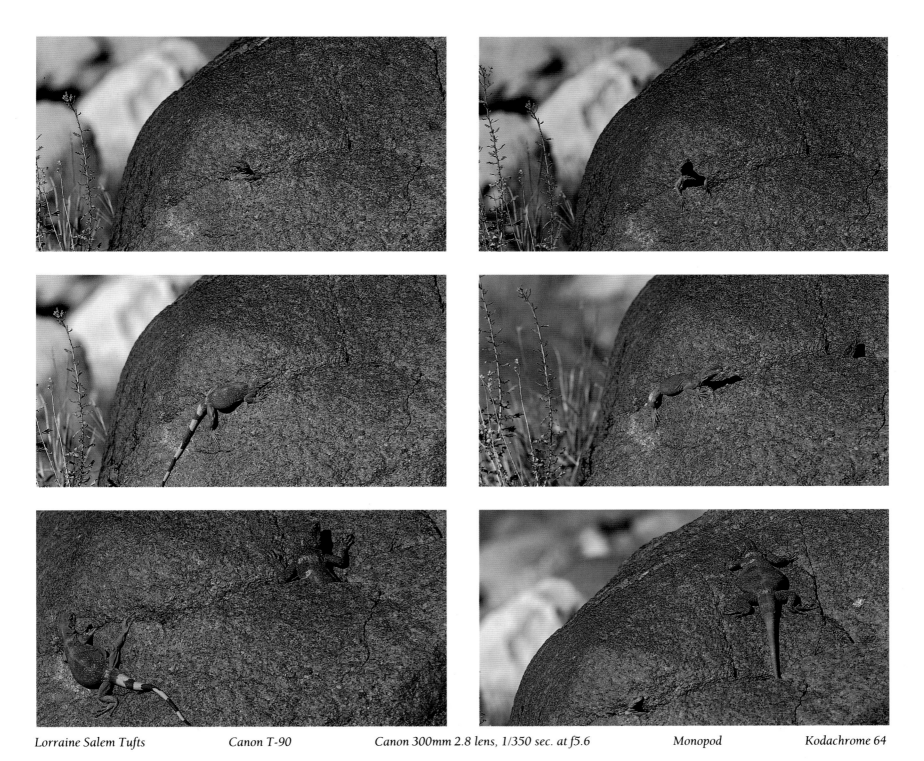

Lorraine Salem Tufts   *Canon T-90*   *Canon 300mm 2.8 lens, 1/350 sec. at f5.6*   *Monopod*   *Kodachrome 64*

CHUCKWALLAS

The photographer found these two in the morning at Tapeats Creek, mile 133 on the Colorado River. The young, reddish chuckwalla spotted the photographer sitting on a rock and immediately headed into a crack. After about ten minutes, it stretched its neck and then forearms out of the rocks to get a better look at the situation. After ten or fifteen minutes more, it completely emerged from the rock crevice and displayed its colorful, yellow-striped tail. After another half an hour, the photographer was surprised when an older chuckwalla peered out slowly from the crack. It finally emerged, joining the other one basking in the sun.

36

R A C C O O N
Lorraine Salem Tufts
Canon T-90
Canon 300mm 2.8 lens,
1/60 sec. at f2.8
Monopod
Kodachrome 64

Henry H. Holdsworth   *Nikon FE2*   *Nikkor 28mm 2.8 lens, 1 sec. at f22*
81 B Warming filter   *Tripod*   *Fujichrome 50*

H A V A S U   F A L L S

These travertine ledges and turquoise pools are familiar to those who love the Grand Canyon. Located on the Havasupai Indian Reservation which is west of the Grand Canyon Village on the South Rim, Havasu Canyon has been home to the Havasupai for centuries. Visitors are allowed to hike to this and other falls on the reservation. Raccoons are sometimes seen in Havasu Canyon, although they are rarely seen elsewhere in the Grand Canyon and never seen in Bryce or Zion.

Mike Columbia   Nikon FA   105mm macro lens, 1/4 sec. at f22   Tripod   Kodachrome 25

CLARET CUP CACTUS
Vibrantly colored, this cactus can also be seen in Zion National Park.

Lorraine Salem Tufts   Canon T-90   Canon 300mm 2.8 lens,
1/750 sec. at f2.8   Monopod   Kodachrome 200

DRAGONFLY
Although often seen near water, some dragonfly species dwell in forests. They feed on smaller insects such as mosquitos and can often be spotted resting with wings outstretched. Again, even the most simple subject matter can render spectacular photographic results.

38

Charles Gurche   *Linhoff Technikardon 4x5*   *Nikkor 300mm lens, 1/4 sec. at f45*   *Polarizer*   *Tripod*   *Fujichrome 50*

CANYON RIM AT SUNRISE FROM LIPAN POINT, SOUTH RIM

| Lorraine Salem Tufts | Canon T-90 | Canon 35-105mm 3.5 lens, |
| 1/10 sec. at f16 | Polarizer | Tripod | Kodachrome 25 |

| Lorraine Salem Tufts | Canon T-90 | Canon 35-105mm 3.5 lens, |
| 1/30 sec. at f13 | Tripod | Kodachrome 64 |

**SPRING BLOSSOMS
BELOW THE NORTH RIM**

**QUAKING ASPENS IN SPRING,
NORTH RIM**

Trish Ramhorst   *Nikon FE2 with motor drive*   *Nikkor 400mm 3.5 lens, 1/125 sec. at f4*
Tripod   *Kodachrome 64*

BLACK BEAR

This black bear was photographed in its cinnamon phase. Although listed in all three parks, they are very rarely sighted.

Zion National Park

Lorraine Salem Tufts   *Canon T-90*   *Canon 35-105mm 3.5 lens, 8 secs. at f16*   *Polarizer*   *Tripod*   *Fuji Velvia 50*

THE WATCHMAN AND THE VIRGIN RIVER

Located in southwestern Utah, Zion National Park contains over 147,000 acres of park lands. The Watchman, a familiar sight in the park at an elevation of 6,555 feet, can easily be seen from the south entrance of the park.

42

Lorraine Salem Tufts
Canon 35-105mm 3.5 lens, 1/6 sec. at f16 *Tripod*
Canon T-90
Fuji Velvia 50

Lorraine Salem Tufts
Canon 35-105mm 3.5 lens, 1/6 sec. at f11 *Tripod*
Canon T-90
Fuji Velvia 50

WEEPING ROCK

**THE PULPIT
AT THE TEMPLE OF SINAWAVA**

The Geological Story

Zion National Park is one of the grand masterpieces of geologic phenomena. This fascinating place reveals in its history the secrets of middle geologic time. The forces of water, wind and volcanic fire along with the processes of deposition, uplift and erosion over hundreds of millions of years have created a landscape of great beauty and intrigue.

Beginning about 240 million years ago this area of southwestern Utah began a process in which layers of sediments were deposited. These different layers of sedimentary rock are known as formations. Each has been created by unique environmental conditions and each is characterized by its own combination of thickness, density, mineral composition and fossil content. Evidence of nine different formations or layers can be found in Zion.

The oldest formation in Zion is the Permian Kaibab limestone. Although not prominent in the park, it can be found in the northwestern corner. Its existence is significant in that, while it is the oldest formation in Zion, it is the youngest formation on the rim of the Grand Canyon.

The oldest prominent formation in Zion, the Moenkopi, is composed of sandstone, shale, limestone and gypsum. Its layers reveal that a large, gentle sea once covered the Colorado Plateau about 230 million years ago. The Moenkopi displays bright colored bands of primarily red, brown and pink.

The next oldest layer of rocks in the park, the Chinle formation, occurred during a time when the land was uplifting and the sea gave way to shallow rivers. These rivers increased in gradient because of the uplifting, and in the process carried away rocks and sediment. During this period, evidence in the rocks indicates that volcanoes erupted, trees fell and ash spewed. Consequently, this formation contains petrified wood along with shale, gypsum, limestone, sandstone, and quartz. Each of these along with various minerals contribute to the purple, pink, blue, white, yellow, gray and red coloring of this formation.

After the rivers flowed for millions of years, they eventually formed large lakes. The deposits that were laid down became the lower portion of the red Moenave formation. Especially interesting is the fact that many fish fossils were deposited in its layers. Eventually, this period of lakes and ponds gave way to a period of stream deposition with large discharges and fast moving water forming the Springdale member of the Moenave formation.

Large, fast streams gave way to slower moving rivers and streams which deposited the Kayenta formation. Consisting of red and mauve siltstones and sandstones, the layering of this period intersected with the occurrence of dinosaurs who traveled across the streams and river beds. Footprints left by the dinosaurs gradually fossilized, leaving evidence for us to marvel over today.

Approximately 190 to 136 million years ago, climatic changes transformed the Colorado Plateau into an arid environment with desert sand dunes. These dunes were responsible for what was to become the most visible formation in Zion National Park, the Navajo sandstone. This layer, which encompasses the great vertical walls and monoliths of Zion Canyon, is as thick as 2200 feet in some areas such as the Temple of Sinawava. Furthermore, the hoodoos east of the Zion-Mt.Carmel tunnel are actually extraordinary forms of eroded Navajo sandstone protected by caprock richer in iron oxide than the underlying sandstone.

One of the more interesting aspects of Navajo sandstone is its porous nature. It allows water from various sources to gather and flow downward through its layers. When the water reaches the more dense rock of the Kayenta formation below, it is forced to move horizontally to the surface where it

Rich Kirchner, Nikon FA, 28mm lens, 1/30 sec. at f5.6, 64K

reveals itself as a stream or droplets of water coming from the stone. This water outlet is called a "spring line" and a perfect example of it can be found at Weeping Rock. There, hanging gardens were created by the water and porous sandstone.

Found above the older Navajo sandstone is the younger Temple Cap formation. This layer of sandstone, rich in iron oxide, streaks the cliffs and walls of Zion red when dissolved by rain. This formation can be seen as the cap rock of West and East Temple.

Once again seas flooded the land around Zion. Limestone deposits created the Carmel formation. The only rock layer younger than this in Zion is the Dakota formation. Exposed in a small area on Horse Ranch Mountain, the Dakota completes the link as the oldest rock in the Claron Formation of Bryce Canyon National Park.

After these nine layers in Zion were deposited, our story continues about 13 million years ago with the resumption of uplift by the Colorado Plateau. This slow uplift, probably caused by tectonic plate movement, forced the rivers of the area to flow more quickly. Specifically, the Virgin River, the principal force of erosion in the park, began cutting its way through the various layers of sediment which had been deposited over these millions of years. After heavy rainstorms or winter runoffs, the Virgin becomes a raging torrent of water which slices through the rock formations.

At the same time as the water rushed downward, pressure on the layered rocks of the Colorado Plateau caused them to break into relatively smaller plateaus. One of these, the Markagunt, surrounds the beautiful canyons of Zion National Park while another, the Paunsaugunt, contains the wonders of Bryce Canyon National Park. Beginning at about 9000 feet on the Markagunt Plateau, the Virgin River flows 8000 feet downward and two hundred miles southwest emptying into Lake Mead.

Geologic processes such as erosion relentlessly change and shape the rocks of Zion. The enormous gorges being formed in the park are a result of the combination of soft, disintegrating rock meeting with the forces of water from the Virgin River as it merges with other tributary streams. Finally, even the pull of gravity plays its part as it works on the joints and cracks of various rock formations weakened by water erosion. It is these very processes which have helped to create this majestic place in nature known as Zion.

44

Jeff Foott *Mamiya 645* *35mm lens, 1/4 sec. at f22* *Tripod* *Polarizer* *Fuji Velvia 50*

SWIRLING PATTERNS OF ERODED NAVAJO SANDSTONE

The History of Humans

The human history of Zion National Park is in large part a chronicle of the native Indians who inhabited the region. Archaeological records indicate that the Basketmakers, an early period of the Anasazi culture, were one of the first people known to exist in and around the canyons of Zion as far back as at least A.D. 500. In the earlier phases of their culture, these seminomadic people depended upon hunting, gathering and limited crop development for their subsistence.

As centuries passed, the Anasazi culture developed and became more complex as more extensive agriculture helped to stabilize communal life. Artistic expression in the form of rock carvings known as "petroglyphs" has been found and dated back to this period. While the Anasazi remained in what is now known as the southern portion of Zion National Park, the Fremont Indians are thought to have at least seasonally occupied the northern portion of Zion. Although there appears to have been limited, if any, contact between the two cultures, both grew crops such as corn and squash which they stored in granaries, both lived in small communal groups and both left the Zion area sometime around A.D. 1200.

Several Paiute subtribes, specifically the Parrusits, occupied the Virgin River Valley south of Zion Canyon for centuries after the Anasazi had left the region. These Indians, who migrated up and down the river valley according to the seasons, existed on wild seeds and nuts, supplemented by some crops, wild game and even lizards. Historical records indicate that the Parrusits supposedly had great reverence for the large rocks and turbulent waters running through Zion Canyon.

By the early 1850s Mormons from the Salt Lake area, attracted by the warm climate and agricultural potential of southwestern Utah, scouted for permanent settlements in the region. When these settlements began to blossom, other Mormon pioneers looked east to the Virgin River Valley for uncultivated, fertile land. Although the Virgin River Valley had been explored to some extent before the arrival of the Mormons, the canyons of Zion and the upper Virgin River area had remained virtually unknown to all except the native people. In 1858, Indian guides finally led a young Mormon missionary named Nephi Johnson, intent on exploring the region's agricultural potential, to Zion Canyon. While Johnson's report was favorable, it was not until 1861 that Mormon pioneer Joseph Black actually built a cabin and began farming on the floor of Zion Canyon.

Several other Mormon families followed Black's lead, including Issac Behunin who built a cabin in 1863 near what is now the site of Zion Lodge. He farmed tobacco, sugar cane and fruit trees. Historical records attribute the naming of "Zion" to Behunin, who took the name from a passage in the Bible most likely referring to Zion's peaceful and utopian environment.

Conditions for the Mormon settlers gradually improved, while those of the native Parrusits deteriorated. The new settlers' domesticated animals

Lorraine Salem Tufts *Canon EOS 5*
Canon 300mm 2.8 lens, 1/90 sec. at f2.8
Monopod *Fuji 100*

WILD TURKEY CHICK

pushed out native game and depleted wild grasses. Eventually, competition for food, water and land resources forced the natives to either move south or assimilate into the new, dominant culture.

The late 1800s and early 1900s signified a time of expanding notoriety for Zion. Influential writers, photographers and surveyors made public the scientific and visual wonders of the region. The publicity increased the awareness of this national treasure, but did little to affect the visitation of such an inaccessible region. No real roads or suitable accommodations existed until after Zion was made a national park, and even those were rudimentary.

Government recognition of the Zion region did much to speed the slow process of creating access and accommodations. In 1908, U.S. Deputy Surveyor Leo Snow recommended to the acting Secretary of the Interior, "this canyon should be set apart by the government as a national park." Within one year, President Taft had signed a proclamation establishing Mukuntuweap National Monument. After a drastic name change and an addition of land, Zion National Park was established on November 19, 1919, just three years after the National Park Service had been created by congressional act.

Despite its newly-conferred park status, the possibility of traveling to Zion National Park was just becoming a reality. By 1923 a wagon road into Zion Canyon was finally completed and it was not until 1927 that engineers and road builders began construction on the Zion-Mt. Carmel highway and tunnel. After its completion, travel and visitation to the park and surrounding area significantly increased.

Since that time, an elaborate administrative and interpretive system has been established to help visitors develop a greater understanding of Zion National Park and the surrounding areas. This system, however, could not have been created without the efforts of tenacious and visionary individuals, the National Park Service and federal programs such as the Civilian Conservation Corps. Each year, millions visit the park and many leave with a deeper knowledge and appreciation for both the geologic wonders and intriguing history of the region.

46

Peter and Alice Bengeyfield   *Minolta SRT-202*   *28mm lens, 1/10 sec. at f22*
Tripod   *Kodachrome 64*

CHECKERBOARD MESA

An unusual monolith, Checkerboard Mesa sits east of the Zion-Mt. Carmel tunnel. The checker-board-looking designs on its surface were created by the weathering of horizontal bedding planes and vertical cracks. The water in the foreground of the usually dry Clear Creek adds a special dimension to this composition.

Lynn Chamberlain   Nikon F3   Nikkor 300mm 4.5 lens, 1/250 sec. at f4.5   Kodachrome 64

MOUNTAIN LIONS

Actual sightings of mountain lions are fairly common in Zion, but uncommon in Bryce and rare in the Grand Canyon. Their fear of humans combined with their natural shyness contributes to an elusive reputation. Sometimes fresh tracks or the remains of a recently-killed animal may alert one to a potential sighting.

Lynn Chamberlain   Nikon F3   300mm lens, 1/500 sec. at f5.6   Kodachrome 64

RINGTAIL

The ringtail is the smallest member of the raccoon family. Primarily nocturnal, it measures about two and a half feet from tip to tail. Sometimes these animals are nightly visitors to campsites, making their presence known by a crisp, clicking sound. They are indigenous to all three parks.

48

B. "Moose" Peterson   *Nikon F3HP*
Nikkor 300mm 2.8 lens, 1/30 sec. at f4   *Tripod*   *Kodachrome 64*

KIT FOX

Rarely seen—mostly in lower elevations—this fox species inhabits sandy deserts and juniper woodlands. Although small in size, it can be recognized by its large ears. This animal is listed as an endangered species.

Lorraine Salem Tufts   *Canon T-90*
Canon 300mm 2.8 lens, 1/750 sec. at f2.8   *Monopod*   *Kodachrome 64*

DESERT BIGHORN SHEEP RAM

These animals are extremely difficult to see in the park. They were at one time extirpated in Zion, but later reintroduced. The National Park Service constantly monitors the reintroduction and recovery program.

Lorraine Salem Tufts   *Canon EOS A2E*
Canon 300 mm 2.8 lens, w/2x extender 1/90 sec. at f5.6   *Monopod*   *Fuji 100*

DESERT BIGHORN SHEEP EWE FEEDING HER LAMB

Lorraine Salem Tufts   *Canon T-90*
Canon 300mm 2.8 lens, 1/60 sec. at f4   *Monopod*   *Kodachrome 25*

MULE DEER FAWN

Early morning and late evening are particularly good times in all three parks to see and photograph this species, characterized by its large ears and white rump. The afternoon sunlight adds an especially nice effect to the face of this fawn.

Lorraine Salem Tufts   *Canon T-90*
Canon 35-105mm 3.5 lens, 1/2 sec. at f16   *Polarizer*   *Tripod*   *Fuji Velvia 50*

MORNING LIGHT IN ZION CANYON

The monoliths and monuments display shades of red with the first rays of sunlight. Orange and yellow hues warm the rocks after the sun begins to rise in the sky.

Lorraine Salem Tufts
1/250 sec. at f2.8

Canon T-90

Canon 300mm 2.8 lens
1/250 sec. at f4

Monopod

Kodachrome 64
1/250 sec. at f11

YELLOWBELLY MARMOT

(not listed in Grand Canyon)

GOLDEN-MANTLED
GROUND SQUIRREL*

ROCK SQUIRREL*

Lorraine Salem Tufts   Canon T-90   Canon 300mm 2.8 lens
1/180 sec. at f4

Monopod   Kodachrome 200
1/60 sec. at f4

Michael Francis   Canon F1   300 mm 4 lens,
1/60 sec. at f4   Tripod   Kodachrome 64

DESERT COTTONTAIL*

(*found in all three parks)

BLACK-TAILED
JACKRABBIT*

PORCUPINE*

Charles Gurche   *Linhoff Technikardon 4x5*   *Schneider 150mm lens, 1 sec. at f32*   *Tripod*   *Ektachrome 100 Plus*

PINE SNAG DURING ZION SUNSET

Lorraine Salem Tufts *Canon T-90*
Canon 300mm 2.8 lens, 1/250 sec. at f2.8 *Monopod* *Kodachrome 64*

GOLDEN EAGLE

The majestic golden eagle has a wing span of seven to eight feet and can measure two and a half to three and a half feet in length. Its legs are feathered all the way down to the talons. Feeding primarily on rodents and rabbits, this bird can be found in all three parks.

B. "Moose" Peterson *Nikon F4*
Nikkor 800mm 5.6 lens, 1/125 sec. at f5.6 *Tripod* *Kodachrome 64*

IMMATURE RED-TAILED HAWK

Common in all three parks, this hawk is a welcome sight in any canyon country sky. It measures about two and a half feet long with a wing span of about four to four and a half feet. The finely-streaked grayish tail of this immature is light in color at the bottom.

B. "Moose" Peterson   *Nikon F4*   *Nikkor 75-300mm AF lens,*
1/60 sec. at f8   *Tripod*   *Kodachrome 64*

B. "Moose" Peterson   *Nikon F4*   *Nikkor 800mm 5.6 lens,*
1/250 sec. at f8   *Tripod*   *Flash*   *Kodachrome 64*

DOWNY WOODPECKER

Smallest of the North American woodpeckers, the Downy male is larger than the female as is the case with all of the woodpeckers. The Downy pair work together in gathering food from under the bark of trees. They share the food resources without competing against one another. This species can also be found in the Grand Canyon.

FLAMMULATED OWL

These owls are extremely small, measuring only six to seven inches tall. Found in all three parks, they prefer ponderosa pine woods. In this species, the male supplies the food and protection, while the female often tends the nest. This picture was taken after dark, necessitating the use of a flash for proper exposure.

Lorraine Salem Tufts
Canon 35mm 3.5 lens, 1/6 sec. at f16   *Polarizer*   *Tripod*

Canon T-90
Fuji Velvia 50

THE WATCHMAN, VIRGIN RIVER
AND FREMONT COTTONWOODS
ON A FALL MORNING

Lorraine Salem Tufts   *Canon T-90*   *Canon 35-105mm 3.5 lens, 1/8 sec. at f16*   *Polarizer*   *Tripod*   *Fuji Velvia 50*

D W A R F E D   P O N D E R O S A   P I N E

In the eastern portion of Zion along the Zion-Mt.Carmel Highway, a dwarfed ponderosa pine
clings to the eroded Navajo sandstone with the moon in the background.

58

Lorraine Salem Tufts
1/20 sec.at f16

PRICKLY-PEAR CACTUS*

Canon T-90   Canon 35-105mm 3.5 lens   Tripod
1/60 sec. at f11

**ENGELMANN'S PRICKLY-
PEAR CACTUS***

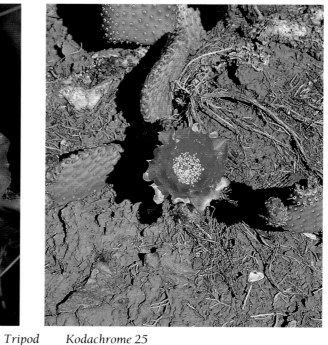

Kodachrome 25
1/30 sec. at f16

BEAVERTAIL CACTUS*

Lorraine Salem Tufts   Canon T-90
1/20 sec. at f22

PRICKLY POPPY*

(*also found in the Grand Canyon)

Canon 35-105mm 3.5 lens   Tripod   Kodachrome 25
1/60 sec. at f8

GOLDEN COLUMBINE*

Lorraine Salem Tufts, Canon T-90, Canon 100 macro with extension tube, 1/8 sec. at f4, Tripod, Kodachrome 64

ZION SNAIL

A magnified image of this blade of grass and Zion snail gives one the opportunity to examine a minute species. This snail is found in Zion National Park and nowhere else on Earth.

Lorraine Salem Tufts   *Canon T-90*   *Canon 24mm 2.8 lens, 7/10 sec. at f16*   *Polarizer*   *Tripod*   *Fuji Velvia 50*

WEST TEMPLE AND THE TOWERS OF THE VIRGIN
AT SUNRISE

35-105mm 3.5 lens, 1/8 sec. at f16   Polarizer   Kodachrome 25

E A S T   T E M P L E

35-105mm 3.5 lens, 1/15 sec. at f16   Polarizer   Kodachrome 64

G R E A T   A R C H

35-105mm 3.5 lens, 1/6 sec. at f16   Polarizer   Kodachrome 64

M O U N T   S P R Y

24mm 2.8 lens, 1/20 sec. at f16   Polarizer   Kodachrome 64

B R I D G E   M O U N T A I N

35-105mm 3.5 lens, 7/10 sec. at f16   81B Warming filter   Fuji Velvia 50

W E S T   T E M P L E   A T   S U N R I S E

24mm 2.8 lens, 1/3 sec. at f22   Polarizer   Kodachrome 25

K O L O B   C A N Y O N   A T   M I L E   M A R K E R   # 7

All of these natural monuments were photographed by Lorraine Salem Tufts using a Canon T-90
camera and Canon lenses with a tripod.

Fred Joy/Light Reflections
47mm super angulon lens, 2 secs. at f22

Warming Filter

Plaubel-Makina proshift superwide
Tripod   Fuji Velvia 50

THE SUBWAY

62

Lorraine Salem Tufts *Canon T-90*
Canon 35-105mm 3.5 lens, 1/6 sec. at f16   *Polarizer*   *Tripod*   *Fuji Velvia 50*

THE NARROWS AND THE MOUNTAIN OF MYSTERY

Lorraine Salem Tufts   *Canon T-90*   *Canon 35-105mm 3.5 lens, 1/6 sec. at f16*   *Polarizer*   *Tripod*   *Fuji Velvia 50*

COURT OF THE PATRIARCHS AND THE MOON

64

Lorraine Salem Tufts   Canon T-90   Canon 35-105mm 3.5 lens,
1/6 sec. at f16   Polarizer   Tripod   Fuji Velvia 50

Lorraine Salem Tufts   Canon T-90   Canon 35-105mm 3.5 lens,
1/2 sec. at f16   Polarizer   Tripod   Kodachrome 25

THE PULPIT IN THE
TEMPLE OF SINAWAVA

A STAND OF ASPENS
DISPLAYING FALL COLORS

Fred Joy/Light Reflections
47mm super angulon lens, 1/2 sec. at f22   *Warming filter*

Plaubel-Makina proshift superwide
Tripod   Fuji Velvia 50

CASCADING WATERFALL WITH FALL LEAVES

Lorraine Salem Tufts   *Canon EOS 5*   *Canon 35-350 mm lens, 1/8 sec. at f16*   *Bogen Tripod*   *Fuji Velvia 50*

ZION CANYON, WALLS, WATER, LIGHT AND TIME

Henry H.Holdsworth   *Nikon FE2*   *Nikkor 80-200mm 2.8 lens with 1.4x teleconverter, 1/30 sec. at f11*   *Tripod*   *Fujichrome 50*

MOONRISE AT SUNSET OVER THE GREAT WHITE THRONE

The Great White Throne reveals 2,000 feet of Navajo sandstone. The evening darkens Zion National Park with only the moon's reflection to illuminate the Great White Throne.

Jeff Foott   *Nikon F4*   *400mm lens, 1/500 sec. at f5.6*   *Kodachrome 64*

RED-TAILED HAWK IN FLIGHT

Bryce Canyon National Park

Lorraine Salem Tufts   *Canon T-90*   *Canon 24mm 2.8 lens, 1/60 sec. at f16*   *Polarizer*   *Tripod*   *Kodachrome 25*

TOWERING HOODOOS

Bryce Canyon National Park, located in southwestern Utah, consists of 35,835 acres of majestic wonderland. The monuments and hoodoos radiate from the eastern rim of the Paunsaugunt Plateau.

70

Lorraine Salem Tufts   *Canon T-90*   *Canon 24mm 2.8 lens, 1/8 sec. at f16*   *81 B Warming filter*   *Polarizer*   *Tripod*   *Kodachrome 25*

BRYCE AMPHITHEATER AT SUNRISE

The foundation of Bryce Canyon National Park was laid down millions of years ago by ancient lakes and streams depositing thousands of feet of sedimentary rock.

The Geological Story

The geology of Bryce Canyon is the story of millions of years of deposition, uplift and erosion. The Claron Formation of Bryce Canyon began with ancient streams and lakes depositing thousands of feet of basic materials which compose the actual rocks, spires, pinnacles and monuments. Before the beautiful amphitheaters and their hoodoos were carved, a great period of uplift created the Colorado Plateau. The most recent geological phase, erosion, continually shapes the amphitheaters and hoodoos of Bryce Canyon National Park.

Fifty to sixty million years ago, deposition of the Claron Formation began. Compared to the Grand Canyon and Zion, the rocks of Bryce Canyon are young on a geologic time scale. They were formed when a vast area of what is now southern Utah was periodically covered by shallow, freshwater lakes and recurrent streams. Over a time span of about 20 million years these ancient bodies of water carried sand, silt and clay into concavities. The materials settled to the bottom in different places and at different rates depending on their weight. The rivers and streams also carried minerals such as iron and calcium carbonate which settled on the bottom of the basins.

Many of the vibrant colors at Bryce Canyon are due in large part to this deposited iron. The calcium carbonate served as the binding agent for the varied sediments which produced impure limestones. An alternately changing climate determined the size of the lakes. It also affected the transfer of sand, gravel and minerals from streams to dried lake beds. Eventually the lakes dried up and, with the carbonates as binding agents, the layers of sediments compressed and hardened.

The next great geological phase of Bryce occurred when the Colorado Plateau formed. About 10 to 15 million years ago tectonic plates shifted beneath the earth's surface. This subterranean activity caused the Colorado Plateau gradually to rise several thousand feet. The accompanying stress on the earth's crust caused a series of regional faults to occur in which the western portion of the Colorado Plateau fractured along fault lines. These fractures formed several high plateaus, including the Paunsaugunt of Bryce Canyon.

Lorraine Salem Tufts, Canon T-90, Canon 24mm 2.8 lens, 1/60 sec. at f16, Polarizer, Tripod, 25K

PONDEROSA PINE CLINGS TO LIFE WITH BRIGHTLY COLORED PINNACLES OVERHEAD

The Paunsaugunt fault separates the Paunsaugunt Plateau from the Aquarius, the higher plateau seen east of the park. One may notice that the younger, limestone rocks of Bryce Canyon with their varying pink, red and orange hues match up to those of the Aquarius Plateau some 2000 feet above.

The last and continuing geological phase of Bryce Canyon occurred when the uplifting and fracturing of the Colorado Plateau changed the Paria River and its tributaries into an erosive force. It has etched its way deeply into the softer layers of the Claron Formation. Today the Paria along with its streams and rivulets receives only low levels of precipitation. Consequently, it has a seasonal effect on the geology of Bryce Canyon.

Erosion in other forms still continues on a grand scale. Rain and snowmelt are two of the most important forces at Bryce, slicing gullies and ridges known as "fins" into the soft rock. All of the layers of the Claron Formation are susceptible to erosion, but some are more resistant than others. For example, cap rock, which is harder, contributes directly to the character of the individual hoodoos.

Annual precipitation in Bryce Canyon is only about 15 inches. Nevertheless, it relentlessly weakens the already existing vertical joints and cracks in the rock. As water flows down into them and is held, it often freezes and expands, applying great pressure. Weather studies have shown that two hundred freeze-thaw cycles per year on the south-facing slopes of Bryce contribute to both frost wedging and accelerated gullying. Warmer water also slowly dissolves the rocks. Even plant roots play a role in the process of erosion by pushing their way down through the rock and splitting apart the layers.

The features of Bryce Canyon National Park are relatively short-lived by geological standards. By human standards, however, thousands of generations of visitors will be inspired and fascinated by Bryce Canyon. The changing amphitheaters and hoodoos will be compared and documented in photographs. New pinnacles will develop while diminishing spires will crumble away. In any event, the unique combination of raw materials and geologic processes that is Bryce Canyon National Park will continue to change throughout history.

Lorraine Salem Tufts
Canon 24mm 2.8 lens, 1/30 sec. at f16   *Polarizer*   *Tripod*   *Canon T-90*
Kodachrome 25

PONDEROSA PINES AMONG THE SPIRES

Many trails below the rim at Bryce Canyon National Park enable visitors to gain a new perspective on the size of the hoodoos and to see different plant species.

The History of Humans

Relatively little is known about early human existence in and around the Bryce Canyon area. Archeological sites in the region do exist, dating back as far as the Archaic period, but none of these have actually been found in Bryce Canyon National Park. Several thousand-year old artifacts have been found south of the park. Their existence indicates that the Basketmaker Indians, the first period of the Anasazi culture, may have been among the early inhabitants of the region. Other remains in the area have been attributed to both the Anasazi culture of the later Pueblo period and the Fremont culture. No evidence exists of these two cultures being present in the area beyond the mid 1300s.

At about the same time, the Paiute Indians probably began hunting, gathering and minor cultivation in the surrounding valleys and plateaus. They occupied the territory for many centuries. Because of their mythology about the pinnacles and hoodoos of Bryce and because of their extensive knowledge of the territory, it is believed that these people had at least some interest in this intriguing place. According to one older Paiute, his people called the rocks of Bryce "Anka-ku-wass-a-wits", or "red painted faces."

White men first explored the area in the late 1700s and early 1800s. Because the Bryce Canyon area in southern Utah was so remote and difficult to reach, it was not until the 1850s that Mormon settlers scouted it for potential communities. The Kanarra Cattle Company first began grazing its stock in the East Fork Sevier River area in 1873; two years later the Mormon settler Ebenezer Bryce and his wife Mary moved into the Paria Valley just below the mouth of Bryce Canyon. Ebenezer, who often grazed his cattle in the now-famous park, took a more pragmatic than aesthetic view of the colorful pinnacles of rocks in his backyard. According to older historical records, Ebenezer reputedly described the canyon as a dandy place to lose a cow. Nevertheless, other settlers in the area referred to the unusual red and orange rocks as "Bryce's Canyon," and the name has remained to this day.

Some of the native Paiute may have assisted and guided the Mormons when they first began to explore the region. As time passed, interaction between the new settlers and native Indians increased. Competition for limited natural resources, especially water, grew as more Mormons settled in the area. Eventually, the Paiute were forced to look elsewhere for more abundant food and water sources, gradually relocating to the west. Several of their place names are still used today.

During the time that the Mormons began establishing communities in the region for its agricultural and grazing potential, others were surveying southern Utah for its scientific and scenic wonders. Major Powell explored the Sevier and Virgin River areas in 1872 before Mormon settlement. In 1876, U.S. Deputy Surveyor T.C. Bailey described the Bryce amphitheaters as "the wildest and most wonderful scene that the eye of man ever beheld, in fact, it is one of the wonders of the world." However, it would be years before a substantial number of visitors would ever behold Bryce's natural wonders.

Many people were instrumental in promoting and drawing attention to this scenic wonder. One important individual, Forest Supervisor J.W.

Lorraine Salem Tufts   Canon T-90   Canon 24mm
2.8 lens, 1/30 sec. at f16   Polarizer   Tripod   25K

**PORTAL ON THE QUEEN'S
GARDEN TRAIL**

Humphrey, began working in Panguitch in 1913 and made great strides in focusing attention on the amphitheaters of Bryce Canyon. By 1918, important local and national articles were publishing accounts of the wonderous scenery, but lack of accommodations and poor roads impeded visitation. To improve the situation, Ruby Syrett, Harold Bowman and the Parry brothers opened modest lodges and "touring services" to accommodate the growing number of tourists coming to visit the area. In the early 1920s the Union Pacific Railroad Company, interested in developing the tourism potential of southwestern Utah, began exploring the idea of a rail and motor coach business. As the stories of Bryce's delicate wonders circulated, increasing pressure was mounted to protect the area.

Around that time, National Park Service Director Stephen Mather thought the Bryce area would be appropriate as a state park. However, at the urging of the Utah governor and state legislature, Mather changed his opinion and decided that Bryce was of national interest. He sent his recommendation to President Harding who, on June 8, 1923, signed a proclamation declaring Bryce Canyon a national monument to be administered by the U.S. Forest Service.

One year later, Congress decided to change the status of Bryce Monument to Bryce Canyon National Park, under the condition that all private and state landholdings would be acquired and transferred to the federal government. Since 1923 the Utah Parks Company had negotiated the purchase and leasing of portions of land and Ruby Syrett's lodgings within Bryce. When the federal government acquired the last of the specified landholdings in the proposed area four years later, Bryce Canyon National Park was formally established.

President Hoover significantly increased the size of the park in 1931, annexing what is today some of the more southern portions of Bryce. An additional 635 acres were added to the park in 1942. This annex created the park's present day size of 35,835 acres, including two and a half non-federal acres. Bryce Canyon did not have its own superintendent until 1956 when it became administratively independent from Zion. Today, millions pass through the park, making it even more critical for visitors to develop a sensitivity to the surrounding delicate resources.

Lorraine Salem Tufts *Canon T-90* *Canon 300mm 3.5 lens,*
1/250 sec. at f3.5 *Monopod* *Kodachrome 200*

COYOTE

Coyotes, found in all three parks, are intelligent animals which have survived despite past attempts to eradicate them.

B. "Moose" Peterson *Nikon F4* *75-300mm lens,*
1/60 sec. at f5.6 *Fujichrome 100*

GREY FOX

Indigenous to all three parks, this seldom-seen nocturnal animal is slightly smaller than a red fox.

Michael Francis   Canon F1   Canon 300mm f4 lens, 1/250 sec. at f5.6   Kodachrome 64

BADGER

Although they live in all three parks, badgers are more commonly seen amidst their seasonal habitat in Bryce Canyon National Park. Weighing about twenty pounds, this nocturnal animal is a fierce and powerful opponent with few enemies except some of the larger carnivores. It burrows for rodents, and will sometimes eat snakes, birds and bird eggs.

Jeff Foott   Nikon F4   105mm lens, 1/125 sec. at f4   Tripod   Kodachrome 64

STRIPED SKUNK

Found in all three parks, this animal can be distinguished by the two white or v-shaped stripes down its back. It weighs from about six to fourteen pounds. The young are born blind and grow quickly.

76

Lorraine Salem Tufts	*Canon EOS 5*	*Canon 35-350 mm lens,*
1/45 sec. at f16	*Polarizer*	*Tripod* *Fuji Velvia 50*

Lorraine Salem Tufts	*Canon T-90*	*Canon 24mm 2.8 lens,*
1/45 sec. at f16	*Tripod*	*Kodachrome 64*

THE HUNTER WITH OTHER SPIRES

The simple beauty of Bryce combined with warm light is all that is needed to make an interesting composition

WALL STREET

Bryce Canyon National Park offers a never-ending opportunity to create striking compositions of rocks and wildlife, dark and light, vertical and horizontal.

Lorraine Salem Tufts   *Canon T-90*   *Canon 100mm macro lens,*
1/60 sec. at f13   *Polarizer*   *Tripod*   *Kodachrome 64*

TWO HOODOOS

Amazing erosional configurations have been weathered over the years. These appear as if they are balancing the dome-shaped pinnacles they support. Set against the deep blue color of the sky, the rich shades of orange which these hoodoos display form a startling contrast.

Lorraine Salem Tufts   *Canon AE1P*   *Canon 24mm 2.8 lens,*
1/45 sec. at f16   *Polarizer*   *Tripod*   *Kodachrome 64*

THE SENTINEL

Hoodoos gradually disintegrate in this land of active geology. The Sentinel stands alone now, its slender shape remaining after a large portion of it was pared away in the early summer of 1986.

Lorraine Salem Tufts   *Canon T-90*   *Canon 150-600mm 5.6 lens,*
1/180 sec. at f5.6   *Tripod*   *Kodachrome 200*

Lorraine Salem Tufts   *Canon T-90*   *Canon 100mm macro lens,*
1/350 sec. at f11   *Kodachrome 64*

WHITE-TAILED PRAIRIE DOG
(also found in the Grand Canyon)

GOLDEN-MANTLED GROUND SQUIRREL
(found in all three parks)

Lorraine Salem Tufts
1/125 sec. at f5.6

Canon T-90
Monopod

Canon 300mm 2.8 lens,
Kodachrome 64

DESERT COTTONTAIL
(found in all three parks)

As with all rabbits, desert cottontails freeze when they think they are threatened. This reaction gives the photographer a good opportunity to pay more attention to composition and lighting.

Lorraine Salem Tufts   Canon T-90   Canon 24mm 2.8 lens   Tripod   Kodachrome 64
1/60 sec. at f13   1/60 sec. at f8 Polarizer

PONDEROSA PINE   BRISTLECONE PINE

Lorraine Salem Tufts   Canon T-90   Canon 35-105mm 3.5 lens   Tripod
1/180 sec. at f5.6 50 FV   1/6 sec. at f16 25 K

ASPENS IN FALL COLOR   EARLY MORNING FROST

One of the oldest species living on Earth, bristlecone pines grow at Yovimpa Point in the southern portion of Bryce Canyon National Park. Aspen trees, as well as ponderosa pines, can be found in all three parks.

Lorraine Salem Tufts
1/250 sec. at f8

Canon T-90
Monopod

Canon 300mm 3.5 lens,
Kodachrome 64

MULE DEER

Mule deer are the largest mammals easily found in Bryce Canyon National Park. They can often be seen in the meadows at early morning or late afternoon.

Lorraine Salem Tufts
1/250 sec. at f6.7

Canon T-90
Monopod

Canon 300mm 2.8 lens,
Kodachrome 64

MULE DEER IN EARLY SPRING

A young male mule deer will spend the summer up high on the Paunsaugunt Plateau browsing on twigs and leaves, and grazing on grasses.

1/180 sec. at f5.6   *Tripod*   *Kodachrome 64*

C I N Q U E F O I L
(also found in the Grand Canyon)

1/250 sec. at f8   *Kodachrome 64*

Y E L L O W   W E S T E R N
W A L L F L O W E R
(found in all three parks)

1/350 sec. at f16   *Tripod*   *Kodachrome 64*

C R E E P I N G   M A H O N I A
(also found in Zion)

All these Bryce flowers were photographed by Lorraine Salem Tufts using her Canon T-90 and a 100mm 1.4 macro lens with an extension tube, except for the creeping mahonia which was shot with a 300mm 2.8 lens.

1/250 sec. at f5.6   *Kodachrome 64*

P A I N T   B R U S H
(found in all three parks)

1/350 sec. at f5.6   *Kodachrome 200*

G R E E N L E A F   M A N Z A N I T A
(found in all three parks)

Lorraine Tufts and Tracey Holmes   *Canon T-90*   *Canon 24mm 2.8 lens, 1/60 sec. at f15*   *Polarizer*   *Tripod*   *Kodachrome 64*

WHITE POINT WITH GREENLEAF MANZANITA

84

Lynn Chamberlain   *Nikon F3*   *300 mm lens,*
1/500 sec. at f4   *Tripod*   *Kodachrome 64*

GREAT HORNED OWL

Common in all three parks, the great horned owl nests in trees, crevices and cliffs. It hunts for rabbits, rodents, ducks, crows and other owls.

Jeff Foott   *Nikon 8008*   *80-210mm lens, 1/125 sec. at f11*   *Kodachrome 64*

AMERICAN KESTREL

Also common in all three parks, the American kestrel feeds primarily on grasshoppers and small rodents. Sometimes called a sparrow hawk, this bird is the smallest of the falcons.

K.D. McGraw   Nikon F3   Nikkor 500mm lens with a 25mm extension tube,
1/125 sec. at f4   Tripod   Kodachrome 64

K.D. McGraw   Nikon F3   Nikkor 500mm lens with a 9mm extension tube,
1/125 sec. at f5.6   Tripod   Fuji 50

BROADTAILED HUMMINGBIRD FEEDING CHICKS

Broadtailed hummingbirds are about 3 1/4 inches to 4 inches in length. They fly quietly compared to many other species of hummers. They usually have two chicks at a time and are common in all three parks.

A PAIR OF MOUNTAIN BLUEBIRDS

In this species, the male displays far more color than the grey and blue female. These birds, found in all three parks, hover low to the ground and drop down to catch insects as they spot them.

1/350 sec. at f5.6   *Kodachrome 200*

COMMON RAVEN

1/250 sec. at f9.5   *Kodachrome 200*

STELLAR JAY

1/250 sec. at f4   *Kodachrome 200*

CLARK'S NUTCRACKER

1/250 sec. at f6.7   *Kodachrome 64*

SCRUB JAY WITH PINE NUT

Lorraine Salem Tufts photographed these birds with her Canon T-90 and Canon 300mm 2.8 lens on a monopod. They can easily be seen in all three parks.

Lorraine Salem Tufts　　　*Canon T-90*　　　*Canon 24mm 2.8 lens, 7/10 sec. at f22*　　　*81 B Warming filter*　　　*Tripod*　　　*Kodachrome 25*

BRYCE AMPHITHEATER

Many pinnacles, spires, monoliths and hoodoos in the Bryce Amphitheater tower 200 feet high. Some hoodoos in the foreground of this picture lack the iron oxide needed to stain the rocks their familiar pink and salmon color.

88

Lorraine Salem Tufts, Canon EOS 5, Canon 28-105mm lens, 1/60 sec. at f16, Polarizer, Tripod, Fuji Velvia 50

Lorraine SalemTufts, Canon T-90, Canon 24mm 2.8 lens, 1/60 sec. at f16, Polarizer, Tripod, 64K

Lorraine Salem Tufts, Canon T-90, Canon 35-105mm 3.5 lens, 1/15 sec. at f16, Polarizer, Tripod, 64K

THE CANYON IN LATE AFTERNOON

HOODOOS AND GREENLEAF MANZANITA

CONIFERS FRAME AGUA CANYON SPIRES

Lorraine Salem Tufts   *Canon T-90*   *Canon 24mm 2.8 lens, 1/60 sec. at f16*   *Kodachrome 64*

NATURAL BRIDGE WITH A DUSTING OF SNOW

Erosion has created a natural hole about 54 feet wide and about 96 feet high from an extended fin of rock. The settled snow indicates the path where water runs down the chasm under the span and deepens the rock.

Doug Sokell Pentax MX Pentax 200mm lens,
1/4 sec. at f11   Tripod   Kodachrome 25

Lorraine Salem Tufts Canon T-90   35-105mm
3.5 lens, 1/60 sec. at f13 Tripod Kodachrome 64

Lorraine Salem Tufts Canon T-90   35-105mm
3.5 lens, 1/30 sec. at f16 Tripod Kodachrome 64

RESISTANT CAP ROCK

**A PORTAL IN THE CLARON
FORMATION**

THOR'S HAMMER

Henry H. Holdsworth   Nikon FE2   Nikkor 80-200mm 2.8 lens with a 1.4x teleconverter, 1/30 sec. at f16   Tripod with monoball   Fujichrome 50

MOONRISE AT SUNSET OVER SINKING SHIP AND
THE TABLE CLIFF PLATEAU

This image has been double exposed so that the foreground is lit and the moon is in a better position. The photographer used a telephoto lens to increase the size of the moon.

92

Lorraine Salem Tufts   *Canon EOS 5*   *Canon 28-105 mm lens, 1/15 sec. at f16*
Polarizing Filter   *Tripod*   *Fuji Velvia 50*

QUAKING ASPEN COMPOSITION

Lorraine Salem Tufts   *Canon EOS 5*   *Canon 28-105 mm lens, 1/30 sec. at f9.5*
Polarizing Filter   *Tripod*   *Kodachrome 25*

RAIN AND RAINBOW IN BRYCE CANYON

Lorraine Salem Tufts   *Canon T-90*
Canon 35-105mm 3.5 lens, 1/10 sec. at f16   *81 B Warming filter*   *Kodachrome 25*

FALL COLORS

Additional Reading

Lorraine Salem Tufts   *Canon T-90*   *Canon 35-105mm lens, 4 secs. at f8*   *Tripod*   *Kodachrome 25*

THE LAST FEW MOMENTS OF LIGHT

Whitney, Stephen. *A Field Guide to the Grand Canyon*. Quill, New York. 1982.

Powell, J.W. *The Exploration of the Colorado River and its Canyons*. Dover Publications, Inc., New York. 1961.

Collier, Michael. *An Introduction to Grand Canyon Geology*. Grand Canyon Natural History Association, Grand Canyon, South Rim. 1980.

Stevens, Larry. *The Colorado River in Grand Canyon*. Red Lake Books, Flagstaff. 1983.

Belnap, Buzz and Evans, Loie Belnap. *Grand Canyon River Guide*. Westwater Books, Evergreen. 1989.

Phillips, Arthur M. III. *Grand Canyon Wildflowers*. Grand Canyon Natural History Association, Grand Canyon, South Rim. 1979.

McNulty, Tim and O'Hara, Pat. *Grand Canyon National Park, Window on the River of Time*. Woodlands Press, Engelwood. 1986.

Beal, Merrill D. *Grand Canyon, The Story Behind the Scenery*. K.C. Publications, Las Vegas. 1978.

Hoffman, John F. *Grand Canyon Visuals*. Arts and Crafts Press, San Diego. 1987.

Hamblin, W.K. and Best, M.G. *Guidebook to the Geology of Utah*. Utah Geological Society, Salt Lake City. 1970.

Woodbury, Angus M. *A History of Southern Utah and Its National Parks*. Woodbury. 1950

Dutton, Clarence E. *Tertiary History of the Grand Canyon District*. U.S. Geological Survey Mono., Government Printing Office, Washington D.C. 1982.

Hamilton, Wayne L. *The Sculpturing of Zion, Guide to the Geology of Zion National Park*. Zion Natural History Association, Springdale 1984

Crawford, J.L. *Zion National Park, Tower of Stone*. Zion Natural History Association, Springdale. 1988.

Eardley, A.J. and Schaack, James W. *Zion, The Story Behind the Scenery*. K.C. Publications, Las Vegas. 1971.

Whipple, Joan L. *Zion Snail Thesis*. Zion National Park, Springdale. 1984.

Bowers, William E. *Geologic Map of Bryce Canyon National Park and Vicinity, Southwestern Utah*. Accompany Pamphlet, Miscellaneous Investigations Series. U.S. Geological Survey. 1990.

Hirschmann, Fred. *Bryce Canyon National Park*. Bryce Canyon History Association, Bryce Canyon.

Buchanan, Hayle. *Living Color Wildflowers Communities of Bryce Canyon and Cedar Breaks*. Bryce Canyon Natural History Association, Bryce Canyon. 1974.

McFarland, David. *The Oxford Companion to Animal Behavior*. Oxford University Press, New York. 1987.

Udvardy, Miklos D.F. *The Audubon Society Field Guide to North American Birds*. Alfred A. Knopf, New York. 1977.

The National Geographic Society. *Marvels of Animal Behavior*. National Geographic Society, Washington D.C. 1976.

We hope you've enjoyed Secrets in the Grand Canyon, Zion and Bryce National Parks

If you would like additional copies of this book or products, please use the attached order forms or call our toll free number within the USA at 1-800-411-6144 or visit our website: www.NationalPhotoCollections.com

Thank you.

NATIONAL PHOTOGRAPHIC COLLECTIONS

O R D E R F O R M

Secrets in the Grand Canyon, Zion and Bryce Canyon National Parks

　　1.　Hardcover $29.95 x _____(quantity) = _____

　　2.　Softcover　$19.95 x _____(quantity) = _____

Secrets in Yellowstone & Grand Teton National Parks

　　3.　Hardcover $29.95 x _____(quantity) = _____

　　4.　Softcover　$19.95 x _____(quantity) = _____

Animals in Action

　　5. Hardcover　$15.95 x _____(quantity) = _____

Shipping & Handling for 1 book

　　　　Within the U.S.　　$5.50

　　　　Outside the U.S.　　$15.00

Each additional book add　$2.00　　　　_____

Add 6% sales tax for Florida shipments:　　_____

　　　　　　　　　Total due　　_____

☐ **Please advise me of future publications**

　　Name_____

　　Address_____

　　City State_____ State____ Zip_____

　　Phone (_____)_____

☐ **Ship to (if different than above)**

　　Name_____

　　Address_____

　　City State_____ State____ Zip_____

Please enclose check, money order or Visa Card Number

Card # _____

Expiration: _____

National Photographic Collections
390 F Golfview Road
North Palm Beach, FL, 33408-3570

NATIONAL PHOTOGRAPHIC COLLECTIONS

O R D E R F O R M

Secrets in the Grand Canyon, Zion and Bryce Canyon National Parks

　　1.　Hardcover $29.95 x _____(quantity) = _____

　　2.　Softcover　$19.95 x _____(quantity) = _____

Secrets in Yellowstone & Grand Teton National Parks

　　3.　Hardcover $29.95 x _____(quantity) = _____

　　4.　Softcover　$19.95 x _____(quantity) = _____

Animals in Action

　　5. Hardcover　$15.95 x _____(quantity) = _____

Shipping & Handling for 1 book

　　　　Within the U.S.　　$5.50

　　　　Outside the U.S.　　$15.00

Each additional book add　$2.00　　　　_____

Add 6% sales tax for Florida shipments:　　_____

　　　　　　　　　Total due　　_____

☐ **Please advise me of future publications**

　　Name_____

　　Address_____

　　City State_____ State____ Zip_____

　　Phone (_____)_____

☐ **Ship to (if different than above)**

　　Name_____

　　Address_____

　　City State_____ State____ Zip_____

Please enclose check, money order or Visa Card Number

Card # _____

Expiration: _____

National Photographic Collections
390 F Golfview Road
North Palm Beach, FL, 33408-3570